ORIGINS

LEARNING FROM GRANITE MOUNTAIN
ANCHOR POINT 1

BRAD MAYHEW

Copyright © 2020 by Brad Mayhew

All rights reserved.

No part of this book may be reproduced in any form or by any electronic or mechanical means, including information storage and retrieval systems, without written permission from the author, except for the use of brief quotations in a book review.

Edition 1.0.4 (July 2020)

ISBN-13:

978-1-953257-01-7 (paperback)

978-1-953257-00-0 (e-book)

For everyone who sees something bad and wants to do something good ...

CONTENTS

Preface — Questions for Firefighters ... 1

— HOLDING THE LINE —
1. Warming Fire ... 7
2. Blank Page ... 13
3. Tragedy of Our Time ... 15
4. Hotshots and the American Fire Service ... 17
5. How We Honor Our Fallen ... 21
6. Remember When You First Heard? ... 23
7. Success and Silence ... 25
8. My Roots ... 29
9. Anchor and Flank ... 31

— HITTING THE ROAD —
10. Back to the Blank Page ... 35
11. Deciding and Acting ... 39
12. Learning from Granite Mountain ... 43
13. Diving In ... 45
14. Back on Track ... 49
15. All We Need ... 53
16. Anchor Points ... 55
17. The Story Turns Here ... 59

— OUR EXPEDITION —
18. What We Will Do ... 63
19. Where We Will Go ... 65

— HARD TRUTHS —
20. We've Been Too Nice ... 73

21. Who These Books Are For	75
22. If You're Not a Firefighter...	79
23. Beyond Bureaucracy	83

— YOU IN? —

| 24. Warning and Promise | 87 |
| 25. Let's Move | 89 |

| Acknowledgments | 91 |
| About the Author | 93 |

PREFACE — QUESTIONS FOR FIREFIGHTERS

How have we learned from the 2013 Yarnell Hill Fire and the loss of nineteen firefighters from the Granite Mountain Hotshot Crew?

This tragedy was a defining event of our generation. The name "Granite Mountain" has taken on a life of its own. We often use their name to refer to the crew, the tragedy, and the aftermath of their loss.

As firefighters, we honor our fallen by learning from them. We can't change what happened. So we face reality, and we find a way to make things better for the future. It is the most meaningful memorial we build.

We would all want this if something happened to *us*

on a fire. We would want other firefighters to do something with our tragedy. To *do* something for themselves and the people who need them to come home.

So, how have we learned from Granite Mountain?

How is our profession better?

How about your crew?

It's been nearly seven years since the accident.

I do not know *anyone* who feels good about how we learned from Granite Mountain.

Not yet.

We owe them better. We owe *ourselves* better.

Our profession has been stuck, and we do not have to be. We have what we need to move forward. It's in the stations and canyons and training rooms. It's in discussions over coffee and warming fires.

It's in you.

But we haven't made it count for our profession. Not yet.

We will.

We are on the cusp of breakthroughs that will drive a generation of innovation. It is up to firefighters and leaders who understand what is at stake and resolve to do something for the future.

That's what *Learning From Granite Mountain* is about.

It's about doing something with the tragedy of our time, and making it meaningful for the generations who will come after us.

It's about your crew, and getting stronger for your next fire. Then the next one. Then the one after that.

— HOLDING THE LINE —

1

WARMING FIRE

Summer 2016. A smoky canyon in the middle of nowhere:

We tied in our burn and were holding the line.

The sun dropped, and with it the air temperature and fire activity.

Gradually, we gathered up near the anchor point, and stood around a little fire to get warm.

Guys dug through their gear, and pulled out peanuts, dented sandwiches, and coffee. We sat down in the dirt, and reclined on our packs.

One guy had a JetBoil and a few had tin cups. There was the usual banter about the best way to make coffee on the line. And the pros and cons of the good stuff versus the cheap stuff.

Someone said, "If you're gonna buy fancy coffee and let it sit in your gear, then you may as well drink MRE coffee from the 1960s." Which was...preposterous. Which was why he said it. Which was why some of us nodded.

"Or gas station coffee."

"Yeah. Or Starbucks." Everyone nodded for that.

We settled in and put on beanies and down jackets, and after a while we talked about a recent run-in with another crew who was burning off. We went back and forth over who was where, who heard what, where the other crew was from. Everything worked out in the end, but I think it's good we go over stuff like that. It makes us better at fire and risk.

We will be sharper next time, because we learned from last time.

I believe: accidents and close calls are not that far apart. There is a thin red line between them. It's made of inches, seconds, and chance. Sometimes you can't see it, except in hindsight. Fire is dangerous, and we are not invincible. That's why we look out for each other, and why we learn what we can from the past. So we keep getting better and stronger.

That's what we do.

Sitting around our little warming fire, I thought back to the Granite Mountain Hotshots. They just had an anniversary. I thought about how they almost made it. I thought about guys I knew that almost didn't. My mind flipped back and forth between images of them and the guys in front of me cracking twigs and tossing them on the fire. For a while, we talked about epic surf trips that were *absolutely* gonna happen that winter, and whose girlfriend was *definitely* gonna leave them first. And we bounced rocks off the guy's hardhat who was already snoring.

There was a lot I did not know about Granite Mountain, that night. Looking at my crew, I did know this: We're not made from different stuff than them. We're just men. Just firefighters. Just like them. We're not immune to what happened. But I wasn't sure what we learned from their accident—how we took their story and made ourselves stronger. I wasn't even sure what the lessons were supposed to be.

I swirled my canteen, trying to mix instant coffee with cool stubborn water, and threw a few rocks into the smoky canyon below.

What *did* we learn from Granite Mountain?

* * *

Pebbles dinking off my hardhat woke me before sunrise.

"Mayhem!"

"Yeah," I said. Before I opened my eyes, I knew the guys around the fire had a cup of coffee in one hand. In their other hand—their throwing hand—they had mischievous dirt clods and pebbles. Ready for the hard hat of the still-not-up-yet-guy. Which, today, was me.

I opened my eyes just in time. Everyone looked suddenly casual— eyes darting to the fire or smiling at the distant horizon, dropping their pebbles as secretly as they could. I heard three hit the dirt. Nope... four.

"Hey, Mayhem... You want coffee?"

"Yeah brotha. Thanks," I said, stretching for the cup already headed my way.

Before the sun got above the ridge, we were packing our gear and getting ready to move.

Last night's question was a dull whisper in the back of my mind. I shoved it aside. And we hiked out.

I avoided that question as best I could. But it kept catching up to me. Like when you have a jagged rock deep in your boot, and you don't feel it because you're working. Then sometimes it digs into the bone of your foot and you can't ignore it. It was like that for about a year.

Sometimes I'd look around at my crew, and gnawing in the pit of my stomach I'd wonder, what if something happened to us tomorrow, and it's something we could have already learned from Granite Mountain.

But we didn't.

2

BLANK PAGE

Summer *2017. Orange County, California:*
I had to square up to that question, sooner or later.

Around the next Granite Mountain anniversary, we had a local fire near our station in Trabuco Canyon. When we got back, I pulled a piece of white paper out of the printer, my hands still dirty. I went out to the garage, and wrote at the top *"**What We Learned from the 2013 Yarnell Hill Fire...**"*

I sat there, ready to list things.

Nothing came.

I underlined the heading. Didn't help. So I underlined it again… still nothing.

Weeks later, the paper was still blank.

I called people around the country — different levels of leadership, different agencies.

Nobody had an answer.

That felt wrong.

I thought, there should be more on that page than smudges of grease and sap and ash.

3

TRAGEDY OF OUR TIME

The Yarnell Hill Fire was the JFK event of our generation.

It was unprecedented in many ways and was a watershed moment for the American Fire Service.

This was the greatest loss of American firefighters in any event since September 11, 2001.

Our last double-digit wildland firefighter fatality was the 1994 South Canyon Fire, where we lost fourteen.

Before that was the 1966 Loop Fire, where we lost twelve.

Never in history did we lose an entire hotshot crew.

4

HOTSHOTS AND THE AMERICAN FIRE SERVICE

Interagency Hotshot Crews (IHC's) are 20-person teams that have attained the highest standards of any wildland fire crew. The media sometimes calls them "elite" or the "Special Forces" of firefighting. But the hotshots I know aren't comfortable with that kind of praise. They don't want it. They just want to get to their next fire.

Although most firefighting units are tied to a geographical area, Hotshots are a national resource. During summer, they spend months on the road, chasing fires as different regions heat up around the country. Hotshots drive, fly, boat, and hike (mostly they hike) to remote locations. They are expected to be self-sufficient, which means being ready to spend the night in the field—to "spike out" or "coyote"—wherever they happen to be working, regardless of conditions. And the conditions are often rugged. They often find themselves working the gnarliest assignments, fighting fire on steep hillsides with just chainsaws and hand tools.

Each hotshot crew has a distinct personality. But most share an old west, blue collar work ethic. Who joins these crews? Some wanted physical work after playing sports in high school, or growing up on a ranch. Or they wanted a way to serve their country *without* joining the military. Or they were veterans who wanted camaraderie after they got out. Or they loved the outdoors and wanted to protect it. Or they started fighting fire as a summer job while in college, and decided they liked it better than studying. A surprising number have degrees they hide. Nearly all of them spend their free time in nature—surfing, snowboarding, hunting, or rock climbing.

THE FIRST FOUR hotshot crews appeared in the late 1940s, with the influx of men coming home from World War II. These experimental crews were created on four forests in southern California (the Los Padres, Angeles, San Bernardino, and Cleveland National Forests). Today there are just over 100 hotshot crews nationwide. Since the beginning, they have been at the forefront of innovation. Due to their culture and esprit de corps, hotshots have earned a reputation as the peak of excellence in wildland firefighting.

But wildland fire is only one niche within the greater American Fire Service.

OUR COUNTRY HAS over 30,000 fire departments. Each one has their own story about where they came from, the community they serve, and the emergency responses they specialize in (including Structure fires, Wildland fires, Hazardous Materials, Technical Rescue, Urban Search and Rescue, Wilderness Rescue, Aircraft Rescue, Medical, Life Guards ... the list goes on). These agencies and specialties have their own sub-cultures—some are more in a silo than others.

Usually, firefighter accidents relate only to a specific

firefighting sub-culture. But the Yarnell Hill Fire defies our usual divisions.

It wasn't a "hotshot" fire. It was an *interagency* fire.

And it wasn't a wildland accident. It was a wildland urban *interface* accident.

Wherever you work, whatever your specialty — this event has something to say to you. Ultimately, it's all about humans and crews making decisions together about risk, and trying to serve a community.

The Yarnell Hill Fire speaks to the entire American Fire Service.

5

HOW WE HONOR OUR FALLEN

After a tragedy, families and communities honor their loved ones with efforts like memorial services, statues, sporting events, and charities.

But within the fire service, we honor our fallen *our* way—by learning from them. We confront the past, and we find a way to make ourselves better for the future. We see something bad; we do something good. This is the core of our firefighter identity.

We don't just do it for the fallen. We do it for ourselves and our future and those who will come after us. And we do it for everyone who has *not* lost their firefighter father, mother, brother, sister, boyfriend, girlfriend, best friend. And we do it for the public we swore to serve.

Look at our history:

- The **1937 Blackwater Fire** led to professional fire crews, which led to the first hotshot crews.
- The **1949 Mann Gulch Fire** led to fire behavior research and training.
- The **1970 California Fire Siege** led to the Incident Command System (ICS).
- The **1994 South Canyon Fire** led to leadership and human factors training.
- The **2001 September 11th** attacks led to an expansion of ICS into a National Incident Management System (NIMS). Today, every federal disaster response is organized under the NIMS framework.

The examples above barely scratch the surface. We could fill pages listing ways firefighters created progress after tragedy. The pattern is: After a major accident, we have investigations. Then breakthroughs. Then decades of development.

6

REMEMBER WHEN YOU FIRST HEARD?

June 30, 2013:

Every firefighter I know remembers when they first heard about the Granite Mountain Hotshots.

I was serving as Chief Investigator on the Saddleback Fatality, in which a firefighter was struck by a tree in northern California. We had wrapped up the investigation and were finishing the report.

As we worked, fire ripped across the muted TV in the background. Scrolling text shouted "BREAKING NEWS" about a hotshot crew in Arizona.

We turned up the volume and listened.

I was sure they had it wrong. I got back to work.

Next day, my phone rang, and I was asked to join the new investigation in Arizona.

Well, Saddleback was essentially complete. The team lead and another team member said they could handle the final touches. Seemed like a plan. With their agreement, I accepted the new assignment and flew to Phoenix. There, I helped build the Yarnell Hill Fire Serious Accident Investigation Team, and I served as the Lead Investigator.

7

SUCCESS AND SILENCE

The Yarnell Hill Fire Investigation took just under three months to build and release.

All things considered, I thought the end result was a solid foundation for learning.

Our work was done.

We passed the baton.

I DID NOT TALK about the accident much publicly, except training small groups of firefighters who asked.

I spent most of my career avoiding the spotlight. And Yarnell drew nonstop fighting. I wanted no part of it. Instead, I applied my energy where I could be productive. Let the report speak for itself, I figured.

Another reason I didn't want to talk about the accident: When I took the job of lead investigator, I knew it would be tough. But I made a commitment to myself to do my best to protect the integrity of our work, and to give my utmost for the future of the fire service, so other firefighters wouldn't have to repeat the tragedy. I made a promise. And I kept it. That came at a high price.

I wanted it behind me.

What made the effort worthwhile, was I *knew* something good would come out of it ... one way or another.

AFTER THE INVESTIGATION, I went home to San Luis Obispo, California, and tried to catch up with my girlfriend and our little dog.

I wrote the *Yarnell Hill Fire Case Study* (released in 2014 and posted alongside the official report), and I focused on other investigations.

I made snowboarding a priority, of course. And I got back to fighting fire.

8

MY ROOTS

Before we go further, this is a good time to share a little more about my background. I'll give you an overview from when I started in the fire service up to today, because all these experiences shape my point of view as I write for you now.

September 11th happened my senior year in college. I signed up to become a wildland firefighter as soon as I graduated. I spent my early years on the Los Padres Hotshot Crew, stationed outside Santa Barbara, California (up by Lake Cachuma). Over the course of my career, I went on to work for federal, tribal, and local government fire departments.

I took an early interest in Human Factors, because I wanted to understand how crews succeed under stress and risk. And I wanted to find better ways to learn from accidents. With a lot of support from hotshots around the country, I built Human Factors courses with names like *"The Fireline Mind," "Dynamics of Situational Awareness,"* and *"The 2&7 Tool."* I proposed and wrote the Human Factors pages in the Incident Response Pocket Guide (*IPRG*) that every firefighter carries with them on wildland fires. For initiative and innovation, I received the Paul Gleason Lead by Example Award from the National Wildfire Coordinating Group (NWCG) Leadership Development Committee. I was one of the youngest ever to receive it.

I went on to earn a master's degree in Human Factors and System Safety from Lund University in Sweden. And I did pioneering work in accident investigations. I have investigated accidents and other events across the full range of complexity, in every Forest Service region in the continental United States. My investigations crossed state lines, regional lines, agency lines, even national borders.

9

ANCHOR AND FLANK

My entire adult life has revolved around a dedication to Human Factors, better investigations, and firefighter learning. I didn't plan it that way. Opportunities kept coming up to do meaningful work, I kept saying yes. I saw the value it had for other firefighters, so I just kept taking on the next project and the next one.

It's like when you get to a fire with your crew, and you find a good anchor point to work from, and you just start working your flank. It's a tried and true tactic of old school hotshot crews. It's called, "anchor and flank."

You might spend a lot of time figuring out whether

to engage at all, where to anchor in, and when to start.

But when you decide to go, you go *aggressive*.

You work your flank and don't hold back. Sometimes it's the middle of the night, and you have no idea when you'll tie in your piece of line. Out ahead of you the fire is ripping and there's no end in sight. You don't always get to see the full picture or the ultimate outcome. But you put your head down and keep cutting. Keep swinging. Keep pushing. Keep working your flank until you tie in to the next anchor point. Anchor and flank. Just anchor and flank.

And at some point, you look around. And somehow…the fire's hooked. Reinforcements have arrived, in the form of other crews and equipment and aircraft. Now they are working the fire. Soon it's contained. Then controlled. Then out. And all you did was anchor and flank and focus on your little piece of dirt.

To this day, that's pretty much how I do every mission. I guess I never quite outgrew my hotshot roots.

HITTING THE ROAD

10

BACK TO THE BLANK PAGE

Summer 2017. Behind my fire station in Orange County California. Next to the pull-up bars:

You can imagine what I felt, four years after Yarnell, sitting on a rough cut slab of red oak behind our station. Holding a blank sheet of paper with nothing on it but the phrase: "**What We Learned from the 2013 Yarnell Hill Fire:**" (Underlined twice).

I had done hill sprints that morning, and was between extra pull-up sets. And I thought maybe if pulled I out that paper and took one more look, something would come to me. I'd spent weeks trying to put *something* on it.

I couldn't avoid it any more...We *failed*. As a profession, we failed to make this accident count for our future. I couldn't find a single way we made ourselves better than if the deaths never happened.

I started crumpling the paper in one hand to stash it and forget it.

No. Not ignoring this any longer.

My mind started probing around for who to blame.

Nope. That's not gonna to get us anywhere.

But maybe we just need to be patient. Good things take time...right?

So, are we gonna wait another four years? No. It's been long enough. Whoever we were waiting for, they never showed up.

Face it — nobody's coming.

AT THAT POINT, I had three options:

Option one: Let it go. Focus on other projects. Choose to move on. I did that before. I could do it now. This time, if I walk away, it needs to be a definitive and final "no." The end.

Option two: Tell myself a nice story. Something soothing. Something that would make me feel better, even if I know it's not true.

Option three: Ride down the path of anger. Be mad for a while, then settle into a nice little life-long resentment. Surely there would be no shortage of grievances to pile up. I could spend all my energy blaming people, ranting about what "they" oughta do. Muttering different versions of: "They're bad; I'm helpless." I could tell that poison story over and over, never acting on the good that's in my power.

Those were my options. Drop it. Deny it. Or dwell in resentment.

11

DECIDING AND ACTING

On a recent day off, I had driven the Pacific Coast Highway 1 to check the surf. Sunroof open on the 4-Runner. I listened to a few speeches of JFK while I was on the road. Even threw on my RayBans in solidarity. Now, sitting on my slab of red oak, a line came back to me from his inauguration:

> *"Ask not what your country can do for you, but what you can do for your country."*

A bit on-the-nose maybe, but the point stands. I could apply the JFK principle here. It was time to stop wishing an agency would handle this, and ask instead what I could do.

I didn't have to drop it, deny it, or drink endless resentment. I had another option. I could *do* something. Or at least try.

I *decided*: I'll own this.

I stood up and walked to my boss's office.

I told him I had to tackle this, and asked his advice.

Through conversations with him and other mentors, I realized this project would require my full force and energy. I couldn't knock it out between fires or pullups.

I also realized, I had to go it alone. I had to reach my own conclusions, free of any pressure or influence, separate from any institution. I knew I had to temporarily leave my crew, my agency, the systems I trusted.

My boss helped me apply for a leave of absence, but he asked me to wait till fire season slowed down.

No problem, boss.

As the day came closer, our crew had some good fire assignments together and some great meals.

For brief moments, I questioned. Did I really want to leave? How was it *my* place to take this on? Whose turf is this, and whose toes am I gonna step on? They were *Prescott* guys, right?

Deep down, I knew these questions were all wrong.

The truth is, they are OUR guys. Every firefighter has a stake in this accident. And every firefighter has a right to learn from it. This accident got used for just about every agenda, except us making ourselves safer.

I had to accept, there was no real precedent for what I was about to do. I couldn't predict where it was going to take me or how it would all go over. But I knew there *had* to be others like me, who wanted to do something meaningful, who would take action if they saw a way.

Late Summer 2017:

My leave started.

Good friends advised I turn back.

Ha. There was no turning back.

One said, "Well, you know what you're getting yourself into."

"Of course," I said.

Of course, I didn't.

12

LEARNING FROM GRANITE MOUNTAIN

I called my mission *"Learning from Granite Mountain."*

At first, I expected to round up a few lessons, maybe debunk a few myths, share a few discoveries. I wanted concrete action points. For example, how should we update our tactics and training, fight fire differently, or change policy?

I figured the research couldn't take longer than a month or so.

After a few eager sessions in local coffee shops with my legal pad, I realized my initial size-up was a bit optimistic.

Learning From Granite Mountain was a much bigger endeavor.

I spent the next two and a half years immersed in it.

13

DIVING IN

I dove into the available data, and I looked at some of the books, articles, and reports that appeared after our official investigation. I also sifted through the rumors. Was there anything solid? Or was it all frothy gossip? I ran down a lot of red herrings and cul-de-sacs.

But I had to know if we missed something.

I returned to the accident site for the first time since the investigation, and retraced the steps of the crew.

Then I came home, put my gear in storage, and hit the road.

I moved to Prescott, Arizona for several months.

I witnessed first-hand some mind bending and gut-wrenching realities in the aftermath of the accident.

Sorrows rippled through lives and communities and gave rise to new tragedies. Traumas cascading into traumas. My heart went out to them.

In their vulnerable state, waves of misinformation flooded in. I saw some people who lived totally in their imaginations, and imagined terrible things. Suffocating in anger and falsehood. Yet trying desperately to bully everyone else into their twisted world. They shoved around all kinds of theories and accusations, and *demanded* I submit and rally to their side. I guess they needed converts. When I asked for facts and evidence, they gave me dramatic *half*-facts and *half*-truths. When I asked for *real* facts, they got angry...or maybe they were embarrassed. Yet they seemed so convinced. I could see how people fell for their strange ideas.

I confess, I got sucked into some super dumb arguments. It was like Hercules and the Hydra. No matter how hard I debunked a fake fact, two more sprang up behind it! It started to dawn on me: maybe some people were *addicted* to craziness.

I had to accept: I could not fix this. And so I decided: I sure as hell ain't gonna feed it.

I anchored back into my mission, which was to build something meaningful *for* firefighters, and *with* firefighters. I had put a lot on the line for that. Every entangling distraction was a rip off to my purpose and my people. I knew what I had to do.

I ditched the debates, and doubled down on my mission.

14

BACK ON TRACK

I met with firefighters close to the accident. Like me, they wanted to focus on their work and life — out of the spotlight. Some had never talked publicly, but they were willing to have a conversation, if it was going to help other firefighters.

Friends visited Prescott, and I took them to the accident site. We ran through different ideas from different angles. Sprinted alternate routes and timed them. Lightbulbs went on as we noticed things we never saw before, and connected details we thought were unrelated.

I travelled around the country meeting with groups of firefighters. I put on virtual staff rides for them, and shared what I was finding. The point was to test run my ideas with them. I also wanted to hear what *they* thought we could learn. This led to new insights, which led to new questions.

I came to see: This accident touches every issue we need to face for the future of our profession.

I threw myself into the research and kept diving deeper. My learning evolved over time.

I talked to scholars who spent their lives studying such topics.

I was struggling to piece together what actually happened on the hill that day, and how. I had to reset my biases and assumptions. I tried to approach with a beginner's mind. I drew from my earlier training in history and archaeology (before I was a hotshot, I wanted to be Indiana Jones).

I was also struggling to make sense of what it all *meant* for us as a profession. Why were we stuck not learning? And where are the leverage points to get *un*-stuck?

I also dove deep into the question of how we investigate, and *why*. I talked to people from every major wildland investigation for the last thirty years. I reread their reports, and I reread my own. What I discovered cast my own work in a new light. Had to do a little soul searching. Then, I reverse engineered a blueprint of what makes some investigations succeed and others fail.

I also had to take a fresh look at our firefighter history, which I thought I already knew. I dove deep into the question of how we learn. I reached out to leaders and heroic innovators from our history, and tried to figure out what made them successful in their time, so we could apply it in ours.

Learning from Granite Mountain started as a solo mission. But I ended up spending a lot of time with people I like and admire. Not just the heroes from history. I mean all the firefighters around the country who were willing to talk about their experiences, and put their heads together, and compare notes. It's not the same as fighting fire together. But there's a fellowship of building and exploring. Take the very book you are holding now—thousands of people came together to help shape it, directly or indirectly. Each one left thumbprints and smudges on it somewhere! I love knowing that. And there's a good chance you'll see your own thumbprints along the way. You might not know what you said or did to make an impression, your role might have been indirect. My point is, this book was born of camaraderie and collaboration. Except for the gaffes, those are all mine.

15

ALL WE NEED

I spent years studying, talking with firefighters and other experts, and testing ideas.

What I found, blew me away.

Conventional wisdom was wrong. Over and over.

We've been trapped by ideas that don't fit any more. As a profession—maybe as a society—our old paradigms are running on fumes. That's one reason our learning stalled.

I'm talking about essential, foundational issues. And everyone I knew was wrong about them. Including me!

But I also came to see: Among firefighters, we

already have the talent, creativity, and resources we need to move forward. Yes, we are stuck, but it's not because we lack something essential.

My focus shifted from WHAT we should learn, to HOW we could learn. Instead of focusing on specific recommendations, I resolved to inspire and equip a generation of leaders.

I know, we are on the cusp of breakthroughs, and this accident will drive an era of innovation.

Not every accident brings a paradigm shift. Yarnell will give us several.

We just need anchor points to work from.

16

ANCHOR POINTS

When you are fighting fire, an anchor point is a sure place where you can go to and start work.

Once you have a good anchor point, you usually have options and tactics to choose from.

If the situation becomes unclear or confusing, it might be time to go back to your anchor point.

Then reassess.

Then reengage.

When it comes to the Yarnell Hill Fire, people don't know what to believe or do. There's been so much confusion. If only we had good anchor points, then we'd have something to work from. And we could start flanking this fire together.

When I realized that, I got laser focused on a new objective—*BUILD ANCHOR POINTS*.

I put away the other material I was working. I sifted through the research I'd poured myself into. I tried to distill the essentials. The only thing that mattered was how to best equip and inspire firefighters to innovate.

But also, I had to find a way to communicate this information. I didn't just want to transmit data—we tried that in 2013. I had to find better ways to engage firefighters. Many sometimes struggle with their attention span, like I do.

I NEVER IMAGINED what went into writing and releasing a book, much less a series. I made every possible fish-out-of-water mistake trying to figure out technology and publishing. It was caveman slapstick. Those are stories for a different time. I did my best, and I'm still learning.

After all that, I am so proud to finally bring you the Anchor Point Books.

17

THE STORY TURNS HERE

It feels like I've come full circle and now I'm finally back home in the shire.

It's been a long road. You could say my whole life went in to it.

As happy as I am to be here with you right now, I did not come to recline and kick up my feet. And I didn't tell you all those stories to entertain you…

We need to *move*.

I want you to see what I've seen. Meet who I met. Go where I've been. Know what I know.

Just the stuff that's useful and good, though.

And I don't just want to dump information in front of you.

I want you to experience it for yourself, and make it your own. To really know where the anchor points are, so you can use them.

So, this is where the story turns.

From here, it's about where YOU will go and what YOU will do.

Here's what that means....

— OUR EXPEDITION —

18

WHAT WE WILL DO

The Anchor Point Books are an *expedition.*

Each book takes you to a new realm of knowledge, and dives into the heart of it.

Each book could be a library in itself. But it's called the "Anchor Point" series for a reason: We will focus on the essentials you need as a firefighter, leader, and innovator.

My prior efforts were like a treasure hunt. But on our expedition together, we'll go direct to the treasure. I've already done the scouting and thrashing and synthesizing. I'll save you the trial and error. We can stash the nuance and complexity for another time.

You don't have to put your job on hold.

You don't have to risk your career.

And you don't have to go alone.

I'll be along as your humble guide. We will navigate the terrain together. I'll pass along insider knowledge I picked up hanging out with the locals. I'll show you old Jeep trails that aren't even on the map. I discovered them bushwacking and comparing notes with other explorers.

Have you ever come home from a trip, and you see your world in a new way? Our expedition will be like that. But it won't be a vague fuzzy feeling. You will have rock solid anchor points.

Anchor points you can stand on.

And tie in to.

And work from.

Here's where we will go…

19

WHERE WE WILL GO

Before any adventure the first thing you do is check your gear. You make sure you have the right stuff and it's working. We do the same thing before fires. And we need to do it at the beginning of *this* expedition. Except, here it's about *inner* equipment. Our trek will be arduous. You will need the right gear if you are going to confront tragedy and learn from it. And you'll have it, by the end of **Book 2**.

In **Book 3**, we head to the Accident Site. You will gain foundational knowledge of what happened on 30 June 2013, and what it means.

In **Book 4**, we go to the briefing room. You will gain

specialized knowledge in how to do accident investigations.

In **Book 5**, we return to Yarnell, this time we will look at the investigation and its aftermath.

But…fire did not start in 2013. If you are going to make sense of the Yarnell Hill Fire, you need historical context.

In **Book 6**, we travel back in time to the 1937 Blackwater Fire, outside of Cody, Wyoming. This was the first wildland firefighter accident investigation. Afterwards, firefighters reshaped their profession. We will see how. Then, we will run through four major accidents, and trace the evolution of learning in the 20th century.

Book 7 brings us into the 21st century. You will learn about the Human Factors Revolution, Leadership Development, Accident Investigation Reform, and four other firefighter movements that shaped wildland firefighting as you know it today.

But wildland fire is only one specialty within the American Fire Service. And the Yarnell Hill Fire was not a wildland fire. It was an *interface* fire. And it was an *interagency* fire, through and through. So we need to look at local fire departments and their culture.

In **Book 8**, we trek around the country seeing profiles of learning and innovation on American fire departments. You will meet Alan Brunacini (1937-2017), of the Phoenix Fire Department. He is widely known as America's Fire Chief. You will also meet innovators he inspired—local leaders who faced tragedy and made something good come out of it for their department and the entire profession.

Books 6, 7, and 8 are filled with profiles in firefighter learning and innovation. You will feel proud of our traditions, which we are all heirs of. Whether you are a fifty-year veteran of the fire service, a first-year rookie, or just a fan—you will never see firefighters the same way again.

In **Book 9**, we go back to the briefing room and bring it all together. You'll learn ten common denominators of learning and innovation, based on how firefighters succeeded throughout history. You can use them as keys to unlock learning after *any* event—large or small—not only the Yarnell Hill Fire. These keys can work for your crew. They can work for the whole fire service.

We don't have to keep failing.

In **Book 10**... Well, you'll see...

By the end of our expedition, you will have what you need to learn from the Yarnell Hill Fire and do something meaningful. Yet, these books focus on principles that are universal, so you can apply them in a lot of different areas, not just this one accident.

For example, Book 4 is about how to do investigations. But it's *really* about fundamental learning principles and practices. You can use these principles at the station and make yourself a stronger leader, even if you never do an investigation.

If you already have some knowledge of these topics, that's fine. I thought I understood them until I actually studied them, and I found a lot that opened my eyes.

If you are new to it all, that's fine too. By the end of these books you will have a firm foundation in the basics.

As we visit these new realms of knowledge, you

might want to dive deeper and go exploring on your own. These books will serve as solid anchor points for your research. Side note—the resources on my website are a good next step. Go to

www.firelinefactors.com.

I CAN'T WAIT to finally share this expedition, not just with the world, but with *you*. And I'm looking forward to seeing what you will do with it.

I know the power this information has. I've seen it in discussions with firefighters in briefing rooms and bar rooms. On site visits and virtual site visits. I've seen firefighters from every background and level of leadership, and from every part of the country light up when they connect with this material.

I put a lot of work into this. But I know the real breakthroughs will come as the natural ingenuity of firefighters meets the truth in these books. As I said before, I'm sort of like a guide. My role is to equip you. The stories that really matter are the ones you will make with your words and actions.

Just wait. You'll see.

In the meantime, while we are trekking together, I'd love to hear some of your "Aha! moments."

If you have something you'd like to share with me, or if you'd just like to reach out, then drop me a line at…

brad@firelinefactors.com.

I look forward to hearing from you.

Before we set off, we need to face a few hard truths.

— HARD TRUTHS —

20

WE'VE BEEN TOO NICE

The fire service has been stalled for years not learning enough from Yarnell. Partly it's because we have tried to accommodate too many agendas.

Firefighters are good natured. We like to be liked. Most got into the job because we like helping people. All nice qualities. In this case, we have indulged too many demands and agendas that have nothing to do with fighting fire better. Or serving our community. Or getting home to our families.

We have indulged these different interests, but we have neglected our own.

It's not just about us, it's about the future of the

profession and what we will hand over to the next generation.

Our job will never be safe, but we can get better at risk. We owe that to ourselves and to everyone else.

It is nice to be nice, but we have to take responsibility for our future.

Nobody else will.

Learning from Granite Mountain is up to us.

21

WHO THESE BOOKS ARE FOR

These books are not for everyone. They can't be.

If we try to please everyone, we will stay stuck, so we need to be clear who these books are for:

First and foremost, they are for firefighters and leaders.

You know the reality of risk, and you live with it.

You understand what is at stake.

You want to do something for yourself and your crew.

These books are for you.

More and more, our fires are interagency events, so are our accidents, so are our rescues. When firefighters are in trouble, it's almost always an interagency effort. In these moments, nobody asks about the color of your pants or the patch on your shoulder. That's why these books are for the American Fire Service. Not just part—the *entire* American Fire Service.

These books might sound like we are talking together on a fire or after work. That's because they came from talking with other firefighters. I hope you read them in the spirit of a conversation.

In this series, I share glimpses of my personal experiences. This is new for me. I'm doing it here because … maybe hearing a little bit about my story is useful for others grappling with the same issues. Also, people are often curious about my background, so I hope your questions get answered. Since we are going to be on this expedition together, it's good to know a bit about who you are travelling with. As with any autobiographical story, of course, the experiences I describe are sometimes compressed and composited from multiple moments and conversations—they had to be boiled down and simplified so they'd make sense on the page.

I designed these books to fit in your pocket. Or you can stash them in your gear when you're on a fire or on the road. Or, you can read them on your phone. Whether you're sweating under a manzanita that's not giving you any shade. Or staging with your strike team at a subdivision waiting for something to happen. Or prepping a class for your crew at the station. You can use these books anywhere.

And I made it so each book in the series would cost less than a beer.

22

IF YOU'RE NOT A FIREFIGHTER...

I wrote these as firefighter books. But I found that readers from *many* backgrounds understand the issues and want to find out more.

Maybe that's you?

If you are riding along on this expedition, and you are not a firefighter, I'd like to speak directly to you for a moment.

You are going into a world you have not experienced before. Most movies and TV shows get it wrong. I've tried to make these books accessible, even if you do not have a lot of fire knowledge.

It's been said the American Fire Service is a smaller version of American society. Our problems are too.

I'll share hard-fought lessons from our world, I hope you bring them back to your world and put them to use. I hope our firefighter stories inspire you, as you love and serve your community.

I invite you to reach out and share your stories and discoveries.

To the families, friends and communities connected to the Granite Mountain Hotshots:

A work like this cannot touch your grief.

Yet I hope it gives you some inspiration to know a groundswell of firefighters are determined to make this accident meaningful for their future, and their crew, and the people who need them to come home.

To those who lead or innovate in other high-risk professions:

First off—thank you. The fire service has learned a lot from other high-risk professions, including NASA and the U.S. Armed Forces, especially the U.S. Marine Corps. Your stories and lessons helped make us who we are.

I hope *our* stories can be of use as you work, lead, and innovate in your world.

To students of learning, safety, and investigations in any industry:

In modern safety jargon, I mostly bought into the "New View," as framed by Sydney Dekker. I even went to Lund, Sweden to study with him. But my books will challenge both Old View and New View thinking, and explore ways to go beyond them.

A philosophical revolution is underway in the fire service. These books give you a front-row seat, so you can watch it in real time.

Buckle up.

23

BEYOND BUREAUCRACY

I did not seek support, approval, or permission from any agency or corporation—or anyone else—to make these books for you.

It's a risky road to work independently. I spent most of my life serving within the system, happily.

But the system can't solve these issues.

Or it would have.

To be clear: This isn't about being *against* an agency. It's about who these books are *for*. They are for you. I put everything on the line for that and wasn't going to risk any distraction. This project had to stay beyond bureaucracy.

That's why I published these books independently.

Who you work for is who you have to make happy. I want these books to work *directly* for you.

— YOU IN? —

24

WARNING AND PROMISE

s firefighters, our future is at stake.

Our future matters more than our feelings.

So, fair warning—what you read in this series won't always be what you want to hear. Each book was built around some epiphany that rocked my world a little bit. These new insights challenged what I thought I knew. It took me a while to test these truths for myself and integrate them.

You may not agree with everything, at least not right away.

But I promise you this—if you are open and discerning, these Anchor Point Books will change how you see accidents. Not only the Yarnell Hill Fire, but any accident. These books will transform how you see risk and fire ... and even yourself as a firefighter.

Anchored in that clarity, you will see ways to take action for your future, your crew, and the people who need you to come home. You'll feel good about how you're learning from Granite Mountain, and what you are doing for your profession.

If you are anything like me, some of your biggest aha moments will come *after* you put the book down. When you are on assignment with our crew, or sitting around a warming fire, after a good shift. Drinking coffee together (or whatever you drink). Because that's when we talk about the things that matter most to us. That's when the breakthroughs happen. That's where it really counts.

So as you read, stay open. Stay discerning. And remember who it's for.

These books will change your life.

They changed mine.

25

LET'S MOVE

I'm excited about the expedition we are going to take together.

Be advised: This will not be a smooth path. I will give you the best I can, but you need to be honest with yourself about whether you are up for it. Only you know. Nothing's worse than a trip you are not ready for.

So right now, before you move on to Book 2 and start this expedition...

Decide.

Are you in?

Good.

Let's move.

ACKNOWLEDGMENTS

This book was born of camaraderie and collaboration. I'm grateful to the firefighters around the country who were willing to talk about their experiences, and put their heads together, and compare notes. It's not the same as fighting fire together. But there's a fellowship of building and exploring.

I would not have been able to even start this series if it weren't for Stan Stewart.

I'm also grateful to the many people who helped navigate this book into reality through their coaching, editing, and advice. Also, thanks to all the baristas who offered great coffee and smiles as I toiled so earnestly and procrastinated.

ABOUT THE AUTHOR

Brad Mayhew served as Lead Investigator on the Interagency Yarnell Hill Fire Serious Accident Investigation Team (2013) and wrote the Yarnell Hill Fire Case Study (2014).

He has led and consulted on investigations nationwide. Other investigations include Pagami Creek (2011), Coal Canyon (2011), and Freezeout Ridge (2014), as well as regional learning teams in the Pacific Northwest (2015) and the Southeast (2016/17), as well as other interagency, interregional, and international investigations.

He teaches Human Factors, Accident Investigation methods, and Operational Risk and Resilience.

Brad has a master's degree in Human Factors and System Safety from Lund University in Sweden. He studied history, archaeology, philosophy and ancient languages at the University of Arizona.

As a firefighter, Brad served on the U.S. Forest Service Los Padres Hotshot Crew and Santa Ynez Helitack Crew, and he has served as a firefighter for federal, tribal, and local fire departments.

Brad was awarded the National Wildfire Coordinating Group (NWCG) Paul Gleason Lead by Example Award for Initiative and Innovation (2007), and he authored the Human Factors section of the Incident Response Pocket Guide (IRPG).

You will find his work in *Firehouse* and *FireRescue Magazines*, as well as national interagency fire training videos. For more, go to -

www.firelinefactors.com

GET ON THE LIST

The best way to get updates and promos is to get on the Anchor Point e-mail list. Go to:

www.firelinefactors.com

NOW AVAILABLE FOR PRE-ORDER

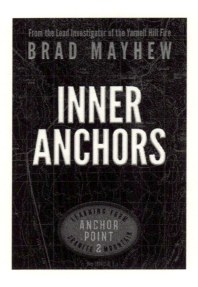

Before any adventure the first thing you do is check your gear. You make sure you have the right stuff and it's working. You do the same thing before fires. And we need to do it at the beginning of *this* expedition. Except here it's about the mindset you will need to confront tragedy and learn from it.

In *Book 2: Inner Anchors* I'll share lessons I learned the hard way—on my own—and developed deeper through countless discussions with other leaders, investigators, and innovators. These timeless inner anchors will unlock learning for the next generation. Lock in your copy of *Book 2: Inner Anchors* today at:

www.firelinefactors.com

NOTES

Manufactured by Amazon.ca
Bolton, ON